OTHERS

I0203645

Sermons We Should Be Preaching To Ourselves

*Cycle A Sermons for Propers 18 – Thanksgiving
Based on the Gospel Texts*

Steven Molin

CSS Publishing Company, Inc.
Lima, Ohio

OTHERS

Cycle A Sermons for Propers 18 - Thanksgiving

Based on the Gospel Texts

FIRST EDITION

Copyright © 2019

by CSS Publishing Co., Inc.

Library of Congress Cataloging-in-Publication Data

Names: Molin, Steven, 1950- author. Title: Others : sermons we should be preaching to ourselves Cycle A sermons for Proper 18-29 based on the Gospel texts / by Steven Molin. Description: First edition. | Lima, Ohio : CSS Publishing Company, Inc., [2019] Identifiers: LCCN 2019002492 | ISBN 9780788029813 (pbk. : alk. paper) | ISBN   0788029819 (pbk. : alk. paper) | ISBN 9780788029820 (ebk.) | ISBN 0788029827 (ebk.) Subjects: LCSH: Bible. Matthew--Sermons. | Common lectionary (1992). Year A. | Church year sermons. | Sermons, American--21st century. Classification: LCC BS2575.54 .M65 2019 | DDC 252/.64-dc23

For more information about CSS Publishing Company resources, visit our website at www.csspub.com, email us at csr@csspub.com, or call (800) 241-4056.

e-book:
ISBN-13: 978-0-7880-2982-0
ISBN-10: 0-7880-2982-7

ISBN-13: 978-0-7880-2981-3
ISBN-10: 0-7880-2981-9

PRINTED IN USA

Foreword

I believe it was Bill Gaither from The Gaither Trio who wrote and sang a song entitled, *"How are we going to get along in heaven with people we can't stand on earth?"* In was an inelegant but honest song about church conflict, and how it affects the local body of Christ.

That title seems to be the thread that runs through these chapters of Matthew's gospel in the final quarter of this lectionary cycle. It begins with Jesus' words of reconciliation that we have simply come to know as, "Matthew 18." And finally, it concludes with a thank you note from Jesus, "Whenever you did it for the least of these little ones, you did it for me." You did it for others. Matthew doesn't spend a lot of time in these texts harping on rules, regulations, and requirements. Rather than the message of John's Jesus calling people to "come and see!" Jesus, in Matthew's gospel exhorts us to "go and do!"

Saint Augustine once said something of this nature, "The church is the only club in the world that exists for those who are not yet members of it." It exists for others. Let's preach that truth this summer and fall.

3

Contents

Proper 18 / Ordinary Time 23
Matthew 18:15-20

Template For Reconciliation

Dear friends in Christ, grace to you, and peace, from God our Father, and his Son, our Lord and Savior, Jesus Christ. Amen.

Every pastor can tell a story of a church fight; some pastors have multiple volumes from which to choose. Arguments over the color of carpeting in the fellowship hall is a popular one; anything the youth director does is fair game for criticism, and whenever there is a question about the inappropriate handling of church finances, even the least active member of the congregation demands an explanation. These topics of conflict are not immaterial; any issue is an important issue for somebody. But these examples pale in comparison to an alleged moral failure, a breach in the trust of a pastor, or a criminal action committed by, or against, a member of the church. These serious conflicts threaten to tear the fabric of the body of Christ, and if the conflict is not addressed wisely, honestly, and biblically, even the most benign disagreement can escalate to irreparable harm.

During the year I served as a seminary intern four decades ago, a motion was made to pave the gravel parking lot of the church. The lot was small because the church was small, but some believed that the update was unnecessary. The conversation was not small. For about thirty minutes, members stood in opposition to one another, and I'm sad to say, it became heated. With clenched teeth and fists, hurtful things were said, and a few tears were shed. In the end, the motion passed, but at what cost? I was still at that church a year later when the minutes of that meeting were published, and this is how it was captured:

"Motion made and seconded, to pave the east parking lot.

Discussion followed."

Seriously? *Discussion followed?* My memory was a veritable fistfight, and deep division. But, like many things we do in the church, it was sanitized for future generations to read. I can't say if members left the church over that issue; maybe everybody just forgot about it. But I doubt it.

Isn't it nice that we can gather in a church, where no one ever fights? No one ever argues in this church. Nobody ever does or says anything inappropriate in our congregation, right? I see you smiling out there; I hear your laughter. In truth, conflict in the church seems to occur at about the same rate as conflict anywhere else in our world, we're just more polite about it. Or so we think. In truth, petty church fights are one of the most damaging things in the Christian church; more damaging, I think, than bad theology, bad music, or bad preaching.

One church conflict expert estimates that there are 19,000 major church conflicts every year in America that deeply scar those congregations. Christians file lawsuits against other Christians between four and eight million times a year. And 1,500 pastors leave their positions every month due to unresolved conflict in their churches.[1]

1 www.peacemakersministry.net

No wonder a misplaced church sign once offered the following message: "Don't let conflict kill you; let the church help!" The fact is, the world does not have healthy practices of conflict resolution. That's why there are so many lawsuits. That's why there is so much road rage, plus the urban gang-banging, and the public sniping in the political arena. The world has an excuse for conflict because they have no role model of reconciliation. But the church has no such excuse; and it is for the church - this frail, often fractured and all too human institution – it is for us that Jesus offered his words in the gospel lesson today. He starts with this simple sentence:

If another member of the church sins against you,
go and point out the fault when the two of you are alone.
If the member listens to you, you have regained that one.

The admonition from Jesus goes on for a few more verses, but this one is the nugget. In fact, I wish Jesus had just ended his teachable moment there. I wish he had not given options B, C, and D. Because what follows then becomes a firing squad of the righteous; it becomes a justifiable piling on the offender by the whole of Christian community. Further, I would say that in most church conflicts, the first step is ham-handed, and then the heavy artillery is called in. So let's assume, for just a moment, that Jesus *did* stop there, and made this the template for reconciliation for the church.

If another member of the church sins against you,
go and point out the fault when the two of you are alone.

So we begin here: that disagreement happens in the church. Conflict erupts. Words are said, body language is projected, and then the feeling of division settles in. But that's not where the damage is done. That is to say that, disagreements - even conflict - are not inherently bad. Disagreement often leads us to deeper discussion and better answers! The damage comes as a result of how we resolve the conflict. Jesus says we must not let the feelings of division go unchecked. "If a member of the church offends you, go to them." Go to *them*. Do not go to your neighbor, or the guy at the golf course, or someone in your book club. Church fights never get settled that way; they just fester, and then they are remembered for generations. Go to them, with your hat in your hand, and have a conversation. Just the three of you: You, your adversary, and Jesus.

When we go to the one who has wounded us, it is not to settle the score, to resume the heated conversation, or to win the argument. We go with the purpose of restoring the relationship. And so, it is perhaps best to give it a few days, or a week, before you approach that one who hurt you. In the intervening days, pray that God will give you clear motives and an honest desire to reconcile, forgive, and to recognize your own contribution to the conflict. Then be prepared to bring all of this emotion and compassion into that conversation. You may discover that the division was not a black and white issue, as you had assumed, but a milieu of feelings, perceptions and misinformation that each of you held. And trust that God will not only restore your relationship, but also infuse it with deeper respect for your sister or brother.

Recently I read a story of a gang member in Chicago who had had enough of the killing and revenge and hatred that persists in the gang environment, so he did the unthinkable. One day he walked into the territory that was occupied by a rival gang. He walked, he went unarmed, he found a gathering of his adversaries, and he confessed that he had had enough. Amazingly, they said they did too! They were tired of the fighting and killing. In fact, as they sat down and engaged in face-to-face conversation, none of them could say for certain what they were fighting about. How astonishing is that? But the story doesn't end there. Recently, members of these two rival gangs just completed the building of a neighborhood playground for the children who lived in the vicinity. Hands that had carried guns and knives were now joining together, carrying bags of mulch, and pushing wheelbarrows filled with concrete, to make a safe place for children who had never felt safe at a park before. The article doesn't say that these were church members, or even believers, but I contend that the Spirit brought them together in a spirit of peace and reconciliation that was crafted by Jesus.

I want to close with a deeply personal story of conflict and redemption; at least the beginning of redemption. It was the first Sunday of my call to a new congregation, and because of a scheduling overlap, a special meeting of the congregation was to be held between services. At issue was, ironically, a new parking lot! As the council met earlier in the week to finalize the presentation, one vocal council member announced that he would be voting "no" on Sunday. Short story: on Sunday, the motion was made and seconded, and "Tom" stood to speak passionately against the motion, especially the process used by the council. After some debate, the question was called, the motion passed, and we all went and had coffee.

I was in the sanctuary, preparing for the second service when Tom came in and began screaming across the room at our congregational president, accusing her of hiding the facts, and lying to the membership. A couple of vulgar words slipped out as well, and that's when I made my way to be directly in front of Tom. "Enough!" I said. "Tom, you need to leave right now. Get out of here." It was certainly the most dramatic entrance I have ever made to a new call!

On Tuesday, I called Tom and he agreed to meet at a local coffee shop. "Tom, I don't know you well, and I mean no disrespect, but on Sunday you made a fool out of yourself in front of members, visitors, and children. You offended many, your judgment of Janet was uncalled for, and I was disappointed in you."

Tom's eyes began to well with tears. He immediately apologized and asked for my forgiveness. Then he went on to say that he had been battling depression, he was drinking too much, and had been seeing a therapist for anger management. All of that changed the conversation I thought we were going to have, and it became a session of pastoral care for a wounded brother. I've heard it said that, "Hurting people hurt people" and that was certainly on display that Sunday morning. Tom was broken. There was still the hard work of reconciliation that needed to be done, but for this one day, his "I'm sorry" was enough.

In his rendering of this verse in *The Message*, Eugene Peterson says it this way, "If he won't listen to the church, you'll have to start over from scratch, confront him with the need for repentance, and offer again forgiving love."[2] Start over from scratch…and offer the forgiving love of

2 © Eugene H. Peterson, *The Message*, 2002

Jesus. You see, reconciliation and forgiveness is rarely a straight line, but on the circuitous path back to community, the shepherd always walks with us.

Thanks be to God.

Amen.

The Subject Is Forgiveness

Elisabeth Elliot was a missionary. She was a missionary to a tribe called the Aucas in a remote section of Ecuador, and that alone may not be very spectacular. What
is amazing however is that in January of 1955, Elisabeth's
husband, Jim, and four other missionaries were mas-
sacred by a handful of the Auca tribe. They demolished
their airplane, they mutilated their bodies with spears,
and scattered the corpses throughout the dense jungle. In
November, 1957, Elisabeth Elliot wrote these words as an
epilogue to her book, *Through Gates of Splendor;*

"Nearly three years have passed since that Sunday af-
ternoon.

Today, I sit in a tiny leaf-thatched hut on the Tiwanu
River, not many miles from where my husband died. In
another leaf-house, just ten feet away, sit two of the seven
men who killed him. Gihita, one of those men, has just
helped my daughter Valerie, who is 3 1/2 years old, prepare dinner.[3]"

She went back. In a mighty act of forgiveness, Elisabeth
went back to carry on the mission begun by her husband,
and she ministered to the very people who killed him.

---

3 © 1957, Elisabeth Elliot, *Through Gates of Splendor*, Harper and Brothers

The subject today is forgiveness, and isn't that odd? In an era when politicians stand constantly ready to sling mud at one another, and nations stand ready to sling missiles, you and I have gathered together in this church to consider the subject of forgiveness. I am aware of the fact that this is not the first sermon you have ever heard on the subject, and it certainly isn't the last word. But it is a word that the people of this world need to hear, see, and experience. The subject is forgiveness. May God bring it to you fresh today, as we seek to be forgiveness in a needful world.

Now somehow we know that we are called to forgive. Somehow we sense that forgiveness is innate to the followers of Jesus. But we also know that we are human, and we are aware of how difficult forgiveness can be. When people hurt us, when people do injustices, when people and institutions fill our lives with pain, we ask "how much of this do we have to put up with, just because we are Christian?" That is a crude way of standing beside Peter in today's gospel as he asked his question; "Lord, how often shall my brother sin against me and I forgive him? Is seven times enough?"

Peter was acutely aware of Jewish law. He knew that three times was the legal standard for forgiveness; even the rabbi would tell him that. "If a man sins once, forgive him. If he sins again, forgive him. If he sins a third time, forgive him. But if he sins a fourth time, *do not* forgive him." In an overly generous offer, Peter more than doubled the legal requirement; "Shall I forgive seven times?" Surely, Peter was expecting a pat on the head and a warm smile from

Jesus, but instead he heard these words, "Not seven times Peter, but 77 times." In other words, there is no longer a limit to how much forgiveness one should offer.

Now there's a mouthful! To forgive, and forgive, and forgive, like there is no tomorrow. What does Jesus take us for, doormats? Like pigeons, willing to get dumped on and still come back for more? It would be easy enough to invoke a dramatic example here; can one really forgive another for murdering a loved one? But we don't have to be that dramatic. We can find enough evidence in our daily lives when the capacity to forgive has been exhausted. How many times can you forgive a spouse for infidelity before you say, "it's over"? How many times can you see your son or daughter abuse drugs or alcohol before you tell them, "Enough is enough!"? How long are you willing to let an employee steal from the company before you say, "no more!" What about justice? What about pride? What about our own sense of dignity; doesn't that count for anything?

In my time as your pastor I have heard your stories of frustration and pain. I have heard wives describe marriages that have never been what they had hoped it would be. I have heard mothers and daughters who just can't seem to get along. I once had a man tell me that he hadn't been back to church because of something someone said to him in the narthex twelve years ago. Twelve years ago!

There is lots of hurt and lots of pain. And the last thing these people need is some pastor telling them that, "You know, a little forgiveness goes a long way." I'm not prepared to say that today, nor was Jesus. When he answered Peter's question, he painted him a picture with this parable...

19

"The kingdom of heaven is like the servant who owed the king ten million dollars." That's today's equivalent to the ten thousand talents owed by the man. When the man could not pay, he begged for the king's patience, and out of pity, the king forgave him. Ten million dollars and he forgave it all! But when that same servant left the palace, he came upon a man who owed him money – just twenty dollars – and he demanded the debt be paid or the man would be thrown in jail. When the king hears of this disparity, he summons the man back to the palace. "You wicked, wicked man. I forgave you a huge debt, and yet you would not forgive another man's debt to you? Off to jail you go!" And Jesus concludes the parable with these disturbing words; "So also my heavenly father will do to every one of you, if you do not forgive from your heart." So also my heavenly father will do to every one of you, if you do not forgive from your heart. Jesus actually said that.

I wonder what my debt would be for the sins that I have committed in my lifetime? What's the price for the lies I've told? How do you put a value on the hatred I have carried in my heart? What's my pride worth? My lust? My misplaced anger? With my lips and with my heart, I confess that I could never do enough to pay a debt like that. And so I tell God that I cannot pay. And God says, "I know." And I ask if God could just ...forgive me? And he does. Not because he has to but because he wants to. And not just seven times, or 77 times, but always. Every day of my crummy, sin-infested life.

And he makes just one request of me; that I forgive my brothers and sisters in the world who have sinned against me. And I agree; we agree to do that! Every Sunday, we make claim to that covenant once again: "Forgive us our sins as we forgive those who have sinned against us." Isn't that what we say? And if we are sincere in that prayer, then we are asking God to help us respond to his grace. If we are sincere, we are asking God to make us a forgiving people. It's not an even trade. But our forgiving others is our tangible response to the forgiveness that we, ourselves, have received.

Author George MacDonald calls it a luxury. "Forgiveness" he says, "is the luxury of the Christian." We don't have to carry the bitterness around any more. We don't have to keep score. We don't have to feel the resentment, because God has called us to let it go. The world can't do that. The world won't do that. But the people of God are called to do exactly that, because we know the value of mercy.

I wonder if there are some in our midst today who have shut people out of their lives because they could not let it go? The hurt is too deep, it's gone on too long, and you cannot forgive. Logic is on your side. You probably have every right to hold your grudge. But the sad truth is that your unforgiveness doesn't hurt them; but it holds you captive to bitterness and misery. Logic might be on your side, but forgiveness is your healer, friend. Let it go, and the bitterness will let go of you. Just ask Elizabeth Elliot how joy returned to her life.

I would be remiss if I did not report one more discovery that Elisabeth made in her visit to Ecuador. When she recovered her husband's belongings, she came across something Jim Elliot recorded in his journal shortly before he died.

"He is no fool, to give what he cannot keep
to gain what he cannot lose."[4]

This morning, before I close, I am going to ask you to do a dramatic thing. I would like you to close your eyes and think of someone who has offended you, wounded you, or betrayed you. Picture that person, or that institution that has hurt you so. *(pause)*

And here is the dramatic thing: I am going to ask you to determine right now that today, or tomorrow, you will contact that person and offer your forgiveness, even if they never asked for it - even if they are clueless to their offense. You reach out to them and tell them that you have finally let it go. And you will hang up the phone. And the weight will be gone. *He is no fool to give what he cannot keep, to gain what he cannot lose.*

Thanks be to God.

Amen.

4 Ibid

When Payday Comes

Dear friends in Christ, grace to you, and peace, from God our Father, and his Son, our Lord Savior, Jesus Christ. Amen.

He walked into my office with all the confidence of corporate CEO, this fifteen-year old confirmation student. Without much fanfare, he announced, "I don't think Mike Stevens should be confirmed." I didn't know Randy well; I had only been the pastor of that church for about four months, but it was clear that he and Mike had a little competition going between them. Randy grew up in that church; Mike's family was fairly new. Was that the problem? "Why don't you think Mike should be confirmed?" I asked. "Because he missed ten classes these past two years, he's only turned in six sermon notes, and he was never an acolyte; not even once! He hasn't earned it." "Wow!" I said, "You keep score?" "Just with Mike," he answered.

Almost a year later, at our congregation's annual meeting, we passed a rather contentious motion to add a contemporary worship service to our Sunday mornings. The old timers in the church thought it was nonsense, but many of those who had joined in the past year carried the day and the motion passed. On the following Tuesday morning, a couple came to see me – old timers – and they were upset about the meeting. "We think new members in the church should only get half a vote at congregational meetings. Their opinion shouldn't be as valuable as those of us who have been around longer." Remember Randy? Yes, these were his parents sitting across from me. Apparently, the pumpkin doesn't fall far from the tree!

In the twenty years that have passed since those two conversations, I am still amused and yet still troubled by them. Troubled, because both Randy and his parents had good reason to be upset. Randy worked his tail off in confirmation; he took it more seriously than most teenagers do. And he carried an unbending sense of fairness within his DNA. Likewise, his parents had been steadfast members of our church for many years. They gave their time and money generously, and they never missed the 8:00 service. Wasn't that worth anything, compared to the Johnny-come-lately's who hadn't yet paid their dues?

The parable that Jesus tells in today's gospel lesson begs the same questions of fairness, justice, and equity. You heard the story; Jesus says that a certain landowner goes out at daybreak and finds some workers to pull weeds and pick grapes in his vineyard, and he hires them. Just happy to have a job for the day, the workers begin their task. But at mid-morning, more workers show up, and at noon, more workers come, and then just an hour before quitting time, workers were still streaming into the vineyard.

Then, Jesus tells us, they line up to receive their pay; those who were last to be hired were at the front of the line, and to the surprise of nearly everyone, they received a full day's pay. I am pretty sure that those who worked the longest began to rub their hands together in excitement; "Oh boy, if they're getting a hundred shekels, what are we going to get? Thousands maybe! This is a great gig!" But when they reached the front of the line, they discovered that every worker received exactly the same wage. Whether they worked one hour or twelve, the pay was still the same; 100 shekels.

"It's not fair!" they cried, "We worked harder and longer! It's not fair; we earned more!" And in a sense, they were right. If they were being paid for the hours worked, or the tasks accomplished, the full day workers deserved more than the one-hour workers. No employer in her right mind would try this sort of thing today. They would be inundated by union officials, lawyers and job seekers. No school teacher would give "A's" to both the student who wrote a one page essay, and the student who wrote a book. I know all about differentiation, but the helicopter parents would go nuts. An athlete who shows up for the last five minutes of practice and still gets to start in the game would never work.

None of these circumstances would be acceptable in this structured, reasoned world of ours. But this parable that Jesus tells is not about how the world works...it's about how the kingdom of God works. In fact, if you listened to the reading, that's how Jesus begins the parable: "The kingdom of heaven is like the landowner who went to hire workers for his vineyard...."

So, when we unpack this parable of the landowner, what does Jesus teach us about the kingdom of heaven? Three things, I think. Three truths about how God looks at us, compared to how we look at each other.

The first truth is that, in the kingdom of heaven there is room enough for everyone. Each time the landowner went downtown, or wherever he went to find laborers, each time, whomever he saw, he hired. Did you notice that? He didn't reject anyone. The owner of the vineyard didn't do any racial profiling. He did not say, "Well, you don't look like the type of person I want in my vineyard." The owner didn't say, "Well, if you can't work twelve hours, or if you don't have excellent gardening skills, or if you *do* have a physical or a mental disability, you will be excluded." Most importantly – and this is a substantial point in the parable – most importantly, the owner didn't say, "Well, if you're not Jewish, I can't let you in."

The Jews were (and are!) God's chosen people; special and important to God in every way. And when the Johnny-come-lately Gentiles come along, the Jews were certain that Jesus would send them away. They hadn't paid their dues. They hadn't journeyed through the wilderness for forty years of faithfulness. In the parable, the Gentiles were represented those who only worked nine hours, six hours, or one hour in the vineyard, and yet the employer provided the same reward to them as to those who were there from the very beginning. It's not fair. It's not equitable. From a worldly point of view, it makes no sense at all. But again, this is the kingdom of heaven we're talking about.

I was troubled twenty years ago when Randy determined that he had earned the reward of confirmation day, but Mike didn't do enough work to earn it. Says who? I was troubled when Randy's parents decided that they deserved voting privileges in the congregation, but new members of the church were second-class citizens. Says who? In the same way, I'm troubled that the Body of Christ is divided in this world by human criteria. Baptists don't think Catholics are really Christians. Lutherans judge the faith of Episcopalians. Christians on the right judge the lifestyles of Christians on the left. Don't you think our attitudes break the heart of God, the way we determine who gets God's grace and who doesn't? There is room enough in the kingdom of heaven for whomever God chooses, and it's not up to us to determine who that is. There is a God and it's not us.

The second truth taught by this parable is that, in the kingdom of heaven, workers were called to work, not just sit in the back row with Jesus. Working in a vineyard certainly must have been hard work; lots of bending, lots of reaching, lots of sun, heat, and cold. Those people in the parable were not invited by the landowner to sit in the shade and watch the work of others; they were called to work. And so are we. So are you.

How have you served God over these past months of summer? Have you fed the hungry, clothed the naked, visited the sick and imprisoned, or have you simply sat in the back row with Jesus? If you have gifts of music but you're not using them, are you working in the vineyard, or just resting? If you have the gift of teaching; the gift of loving Christ and loving children, and you know that this congregation needs teachers, will you show up for work? If you have ample income to meet your every need, will you invest it in kingdom work, or invest it only in yourself? Please, I'm not scolding us, nor am I ridiculing us;

but if the kingdom of heaven is like the workers in the landowner's vineyard, what are we doing in this world, for heaven's sake?

Having said that, let me tell you the third truth revealed in this parable, a truth that is characteristically biblical. The workers in the parable did not earn their pay by how many hours they worked. They didn't earn their wage by how many bushels of grapes they picked. If they had – if their reward was based on work done – then the landowner should have rewarded each of them individually for what they accomplished. But no, they trusted the landowner's word, and they followed him to the vineyard. And when payday came, the owner made good on his promise.

In the same way, we do not gain the kingdom of heaven by the good works we do in this world. We gain the kingdom by heeding the call of the landowner to follow. By trusting in the landowner's promise, we gain it all. Some do more, some give more, and some have been around longer than others. If we insist on comparing our contribution to theirs, then we become Randy, the fifteen-year-old who kept score; who decided who's in, and who's out, and what is fair. If God was fair, none of us would make it. If God was rigidly just, none of us would meet the standard of righteousness. God is not fair, God is gracious; and because of this, we have the promise of eternal life.

I will close with a story Pastor Frank Harrington once told of being a judge at the Special Olympics in Atlanta. In the 100-meter dash, ten-year-old boys and girls lined up to start the race. When the gun sounded, they bolted, but after only a few strides, one of the girls went down. The boy in the next lane glanced at her on the ground, and then he did a surprising thing; he stopped. He stopped and helped her to her feet. Another racer also stopped to help. And then another, and another. Pretty soon, all eight athletes – special athletes in every way – stopped to help the fallen runner. Then they walked, arm in arm, across the finish line together. Stunned spectators and proud parents, all with tears flowing, watched as all of the racers received the same prize: first place.[5]

In the kingdom, I think that describes the Body of Christ. We are not competitors, nor are we adversaries. We are fellow travelers on the road. The God of grace is our greatest cheerleader. When payday comes, so too will eternal life with the Savior, and nothing else will matter. But how shall we live until that day?

Thanks be to God.

Amen.

---

5 W. Frank Harrington was senior pastor of Peachtree Presbyterian, the largest PC-USA in America, for more than 25 years. Upon his death in 1999, Harrington's sermon manuscripts and videos were donated to Columbia Theological Seminary, Decatur, Georgia. You can find them at: www.ctsnet. edu

Polite Disobedience

Dear friends in Christ, grace, mercy and peace, from God our Father, and his Son, our Lord and Savior, Jesus Christ. Amen.

The title of this sermon is "Polite Disobedience." I was going to call it "The Gospel of Eddie Haskel" but that reference is from so long ago, I figured half of you are too young to know of it, and the other half of you are too old to remember it!

Eddie Haskel was the best friend of Wally Cleaver on the "Leave it to Beaver" TV show of the 1950's. Eddie was the kind of kid you'd just kind of like to punch in the nose sometimes. Because whenever he was around adults, he was as polite and charming, and as sweet as sweet could be. "Good evening Mr. Cleaver, good evening Mrs. Cleaver. My, that's a lovely dress you're wearing tonight, Mrs. Cleaver." But when the adults left the room, Eddie turned into a jerk! "Wally, your parents are so lame, and what's up with the polka dot dress, anyway?"

When Eddie disobeyed, he did it in the nicest way. When he rebelled, all of the adults thought he was still kind, and charming, and, well...polite. You have known people like that, and so have I. To our faces, they are respectful and agreeable and loyal, but then we hear from other sources that they have been critical of us, that they didn't follow through on the things they were supposed to do, and if fact, never planned to.

Well, Jesus knew people like this, too. Some of them were called The Pharisees. They were religious leaders in Israel, admired and respected by all, saying the right things at the right time, and appearing to be just about perfect. They had all the answers, and knew all the rules, and they preached all the rules to the people. But the fact is, they didn't follow the rules themselves. The Pharisees found ways to skirt religious rules; they found loopholes and exceptions for themselves, but criticized others for not keeping the rules. They were hypocrites, that is what they were.

And these are the people to whom Jesus is speaking in today's gospel lesson; the Pharisees. They're questioning Jesus' authority. They're wondering why he can say and do the things he does, but Jesus sees right through them, these first century Eddie Haskels.

"Let me tell you a story," Jesus begins. A farmer has two sons, and one morning he asks them both to go out and work in the vineyard. One says no immediately. "I will not go work in the vineyard; I'm busy, I have other plans, it doesn't fit into my schedule." But the other son responds in the most respectful voice, "I will go, sir." In the Greek, the son calls his father, *Lord*. "I will go, Lord." (My, what a nice dress you're wearing tonight, Mrs. Cleaver!).

The second son does not go to work in the vineyard that day; in fact, he never intended to work in the vineyard, but his charm got him out of the house. He dodged a bullet and he could always come up with an excuse later.

But the first son has a change of heart. He had remorse for the way he had answered his father, so he went and worked in the fields.

When Jesus concluded his parable, he asked the Pharisees "Which of the sons, do you think, did the will of his father?" And all agreed that it was the first one. And then Jesus lowered the boom! "And I'm telling you that tax-collectors and prostitutes will be getting into heaven before you." And the Pharisees were stunned! They didn't think tax collectors and prostitutes were getting into heaven at all, and now Jesus is saying they will be first in line. And it wasn't long after hearing this parable that the Jews began making plans to kill Jesus.

But the parable didn't die; it has been preserved in scripture to now be read by the Pharisees of the twenty first century. Now we are the ones asked by Jesus to decide which of the two sons is doing the father's will. Now we decide which one's going to heaven. And it is fitting that we are asked to make that pronouncement, because we do it all the time. We judge people for the way they look and the things they say and do. But we're polite about it! We don't condemn them to their face; we wait until we're back with other Pharisees like us, and then we judge. And here is what we often decide:

> *If they are prison inmates, they're not going to heaven*
>
> *If they have an Arab-sounding name, they aren't going to heaven*
>
> *If their church headquarters is in Salt Lake City, they aren't going to heaven*
>
> *If they are the wrong sexual orientation, they aren't going to heaven*

*If they're a drunk, a gambler, an addict or a Packer fan,
they aren't going to heaven*

These are the tax-collectors and prostitutes of the twenty-first century, and their disobedience is bold, blatant, and unacceptable.

So, what about us? We're polite; we dress up on Sunday mornings and go to church. We smile a lot, and sing hymns and pray prayers, and give money, and enroll our kids in Sunday school. And all of this is good! This is exactly what God wants us to do on Sunday mornings and Wednesday nights, but this is not the vineyard. In the church, surrounded by others just like us, is not the vineyard. Out there; that's the vineyard. That is the field where God has called us to work.

And even inside the church, we often emulate the second son in the parable:

Parents and sponsors bring their children to the front and politely promise to raise these children in worship and Sunday school, and often, they do not. Rich Melheim says we should rent large stadiums and hire dynamic speakers and then gather these baptism sponsors together and call it "Promise Breakers."

Two weeks from now, 24 confirmands will stand up and politely confess that they will continue to gather among God's people, to hear the word, share in communion, and proclaim Christ's love. But if the national statistics are accurate, 50% of them will never return.

We confess each Sunday that everything on earth belongs to God; even our homes, and our money, and our children belong to God, and it's all on loan to us. But then we are offended when God asks for some of it back for the work of the church.

We pray each week, asking God to forgive us in the same way we have forgiven others, *(forgive us our trespasses as we forgive those who trespass against us)* and we fail to realize that we have not forgiven others at all.

All of this is to suggest that most of us have perfected the art of polite disobedience. We say one thing to God, and we do another. And then we condemn those whose lives are rougher around the edges than ours are. Essentially, we have politely lied to God, and they have belligerently told the truth to God, and we think we're better than them. And this parable of the two sons tells us that we're not.

Now here's the good news: being politely disobedient does not exclude us from the kingdom of God. Last week, I reminded you that some will be first and some will be last, but none will be absent. And that same truth is evident in today's gospel. God's grace is wide enough to accept all of us, even the Pharisees, if we trust his gift of forgiveness. It doesn't mean that disobedience is okay. It doesn't mean that our selfish deeds and unkind words make God smile. It simply means that all of us – all of us – are on a journey, but all of us – all of us – are in the family - even the Pharisees.

I close with this. Twenty years ago, I took a group of teenagers from Salem, Oregon, to Ensenada, Mexico, to work on a Habitat for Humanity project. From the moment we left Salem, Diane was a problem. She refused to listen when I spoke, she refused to work on the Habitat house, she defied curfew at night, she fought with the other girls and she made out with every boy from the other church that went with us. On the last day in Mexico, she said "You're not the boss of me." I almost scheduled her funeral on the spot! And when we got back to Salem, she went off to college, and I moved a year later, and I never saw her again.

Last year, I received an envelope postmarked Anchorage, Alaska, and the note inside said this:

Dear Pastor Steve,

I don't know if you'll remember me, but the summer after high school, you took us on a mission trip to Mexico. (Oh, I remembered her!) *I can't believe how mean I was to you, and to everyone else. I am amazed that you didn't send me home before the week ended* (actually, we talked about that but we couldn't afford the one-way ticket). *I am embarrassed now to even remember it.*

The reason I am writing you is to apologize, and to thank you. Looking back, that week opened my eyes and changed my life. In college, I came to know Jesus Christ. I married a wonderful Christian man, and now we have two small children and I'm teaching Sunday school at a Lutheran Church in Anchorage. I guess it just takes some of us a little while longer to see the light.

In Christ's Love,

Diane

And meanwhile…Matthew wrote, "A certain man had two children, and went to the first and said 'Go to work in the vineyard today' and she answered 'I will not' but later changed her mind. And Jesus asked which one did the father's will? And the people said "The first." And the name of that child was…*us.*

Thanks be to God.

Amen.

Speaking Of Us

Dear friends in Christ, grace, mercy and peace, from God our Father, and his Son, our Lord and Savior, Jesus Christ. Amen.

He was, by all accounts, a successful man. This builder of fine homes in an upscale American suburb was known to all as a creative craftsman, a shrewd businessman, a fair-minded employer, and a generous benefactor. But he was aging now, and before he set out for Florida for the winter, he approached his top superintendent and told him that he was retiring. "I want you to build me a home, the finest home this company has ever built. Spare no expense, use the finest materials, employ the most gifted tradesmen, and build me a masterpiece before I come home next spring."

The next day, the superintendent set out to build that home, but not exactly to orders. If his boss was retiring, that meant he would be losing his job, so he needed to pad his own savings account, lest he be destitute. He ordered inferior concrete blocks for the foundation, but charged the builder for premium blocks, and he pocketed the difference. He hired inexperienced carpenters, plumbers, electricians, roofers, and landscapers, but he charged his boss wages that would be paid to master craftsmen, and he put the difference in his own bank account. He installed cheap appliances and lighting, insufficient insulation, inferior carpet, and drafty windows, and he skimmed a tidy sum off the top for himself. In the spring, when the home was finished, it looked spectacular; it was the signature home in the neighborhood, and the only thing that made the superintendent happier than how the project looked was the bottom line in his personal bank account, which had grown by hundreds of thousands of dollars that winter.

When the elderly business owner arrived home from Florida that spring, he toured this home fit for a king, and he was ecstatic. The superintendent handed him the keys and thanked his boss for the privilege of working for him all these years. And then the owner did an unthinkable thing: he said to the superintendent, "You have been a trusted friend and a loyal partner in my business for all of these years; you deserve a home like this." And he handed him the keys.

Greed is what that story is about, and greed is everywhere. This week, we have all had front row seats to witness greed at its best...or should I say, at its worst? Governmental leaders have dominated the news cycles recently for using their positions of power to increase their own personal wealth. CEOs of corporations earn multiple times what their boots on the ground employees earn for their labor, but if shareholders are happy, that's what matters. Wealth managers steal from their investors. Investors take enormous risk to become richer. Banks take advantage of naïve clients and charge unfair interest rates.

Those are the casualties of greed. And these are just the highlights. Examples of human selfishness and greed surround us everyday. And that's why this parable that Jesus tells us in Matthew's gospel is so timely and so relevant; because as that wise homebuilder knew the heart of his superintendent, so Jesus knows the selfish condition of our hearts, and he desires that we change our ways. So here's the story that Jesus told:

A certain landowner decided to plant a vineyard; he hauled in the finest soil, he planted the finest grapes, he built a wall to protect his crops, and a tower to watch over them. Then he leased the vineyard out to tenants; not an unusual practice in farming, even today. A farmer family I got to know in South Dakota owned 1,000 acres of rich land along the Missouri River, and they grew popcorn; if you ever ate Jolly Time Popcorn, you may have been munching some of Larry and Gwen's crop. But Larry died and Gwen couldn't actively raise and harvest a crop any longer, so she leased out those thousand acres. She might have charged so much per acre for rent, or she might have required a percentage of the harvest. Either way, every year, Gwen got a check, just like the landowner in the parable.

But in the parable Jesus told, the renters got greedy. They looked at all the effort they invested in growing the crop, caring for the vines, harvesting the grapes, taking them to market, and yet they resented the fact that the landowner received just as much from the sale of the grapes as the workers did. "Not fair!" they cried. We deserve better. No, they didn't, but their greed told them that they did, so the next time the associate manager of the landowner cames for the check, they killed him. And then, when the assistant manager of the landowner came to collect the rent, they killed her. And when the head manager arrived, they beat him up and left him to die. Finally, the landowner had had enough, and he reasons, "If I send my son, surely they will respect him." Wrong again, because now the renters believed that if they killed the son, the vineyard would be theirs. How in the world did they come up with that conclusion?

Jesus concluded the parable by asking the Pharisees "When the owner of that vineyard finally shows up, what do you think he will do with those renters?" And the Pharisees responded in one voice, "He will kill the renters for their greed, take the vineyard away from them, and give it to someone else who will be faithful in paying the rent." "Right you are!" Jesus says, "And God will do the same thing to you!"

I love the last line of the text. "When the Pharisees realized that Jesus was speaking of them, they wanted to arrest him and made plans to kill him. 'He was speaking of us' they said." Well, duh! But that's how it is with greed, if we're good at it, we don't think we're being greedy; we're simply taking what we have rightly earned. And if we're really good at it, we point to others and blame them for their selfish, unethical, and hurtful behavior.

Who is to blame for the Wall Street fiasco; was it the greedy lenders? "You're darn right it was the predatory lenders!" Who's to blame for the high cost of a gallon of gasoline? Well Exxon, of course! Who is to blame for the high cost of health care; the insurance companies? Yes! It's certainly not our fault; our hands are clean, our motives are always pure, our actions are always selfless and benevolent. Well, here's some breaking news from the Bible, folks: He was speaking of us, too. Jesus was speaking of us in the parable of the wicked tenants. In fact, we are present in every parable that Jesus ever told. German theologian Helmut Thielicke said that we will never understand those parables until we see ourselves starring in them.[6] People, the wicked renters are us. We have been placed in the lushest vineyard in the world. We have essentially been given everything we need for life; food, clothing, shelter, meaningful work, family, friends, church, and community. And it ought to be enough; for some it is, but for many, it is not. So we get greedy and ask for more. We structure our lives so that we can accumulate more stuff, more success, more fame, more power, and more trophies.

And every once in awhile, the landowner shows up and asks, "What about me?" Whaddaya mean, 'what about you?' And the landowner replies; "I have given you all of this to use, and now I've come for the rent." And we kill him. We still his voice and ignore his claim upon our lives. We refuse to acknowledge that he is the source of everything we have, and we insist that, no, it is our own doing. But now the rent comes due.

The rent God seeks from us is our time. There are 168 hours a week, and yet we begrudge being asked to spend one quiet hour in worship each week to give thanks.

The rent God seeks is our abilities. We have been gifted with amazing talents, skills and abilities, but we often dismiss what we can do, and we covet someone else's talent.

6 © 1959, *The Waiting Father*, Helmut Thielicke

The rent God seeks is a portion of our money. Everything we have in this world actually belongs to God, and is simply on loan to us. He asks that we wisely use what we have, and return a portion of it to the work of the kingdom. But we forget to pay the rent, or we refuse to pay the rent, and then complain that all the church ever speaks about is money.

The rent God seeks is righteous living, but sin and greed and selfishness are the weeds of our lives. God can accept that; he knows we're sinners. But what we fail to do is confess our shortcomings to this gracious God. We hide our sin, we justify our sin, we compare our sins to others and take pride that we sin less. And God cries out "How can I forgive you if you insist that there is nothing to forgive?"

In this parable, Jesus is not speaking to us. That's too vague. Jesus is speaking to *you*. No, Jesus is speaking to me. I am the wicked tenant personified. But I have met the landowner and find him to be a compassionate and gracious God. He gives me a second chance. He gives me more time, but his patience will not last forever. I vow today to take a look at my life and to confess and correct the greed that lies within me. And I invite my fellow renters to join me. The vineyard is ours to use; the landowner is ours to love. And his is the purpose to forgive us.

Thanks be to God.

Amen.

Welcome To The Party!

Dear friends in Christ, grace to you, and peace, from God our Father, and his Son, our Lord and Savior, Jesus Christ. Amen.

Not long ago, our daughter Kindra married Chris in a wonderful celebration. If you have ever planned a wedding with a daughter, then you know the love/hate relationship that can develop during that year! But on the day of the wedding, when all of the details have been settled, that day is glorious!

One of the things I vividly recall about our family wedding was the reception. We sent out invitations for 220 people, but only 200 people came. Now why would 20 people decline our invitation? Hey, we're nice people. Kindra was a beautiful bride, and the food at the Lowell Inn was fabulous! And while I was disappointed that some of our friends did not attend, I am pleased to say that nobody was killed for their absence, and no guests were thrown out into the darkness because they wore a T-shirt and flip-flops.

That makes the story in our gospel lesson today a difficult parable. It is a terrible parable, in fact. So let me review the words from Matthew's gospel, and then wonder with you why this wedding feast ended so badly.

Jesus said that the kingdom of heaven is like a certain king who threw a wedding feast for his son. The invitations went out, but they weren't really invitations at all; they were commands. People were being summoned to the royal palace. When all of the guests sent back their regrets, another summons was hand-delivered by the king's servants, this time describing the event more fully. "Why wouldn't you want to come? I'm your king. The bride will be beautiful, and already we're decorating the palace and cooking up veal and mashed potatoes. You come!" But the invited guests would not attend, and in fact, they made fun of the king and his invitation and just for an exclamation point, they killed the messengers.

The king was livid. Apparently, you don't turn down a royal invitation, and you surely don't kill his servants! So the king sent troops to annihilate the ungrateful subjects, and then he burned their city. He instructed the servants to go out into the streets and invite to the wedding feast anyone they could find; the homeless, the rejected, the nobodies; all were welcome at his table. And when the palace was filled to overflowing, the party began. But one of the guests was not dressed appropriately. Even though the king handed out wedding robes to all the guests, one character decided against putting it on, and the king got angry all over again. He had that guest bound and gagged, and thrown into the wilderness. Wow!

This story disturbs me, and I expect that it disturbs you as well. Not just because the king seems so brutal toward those who declined his invitation, but also because Jesus announced that this is what the kingdom of heaven is like. Seriously? Seriously? The kingdom of heaven is a place where people are killed for not accepting God's invitation? And the king in heaven is so enraged that anyone who doesn't follow the dress code will be kicked out? That doesn't sound like the God of whom I have preached for 35 years. So I have struggled mightily this week trying to make sense of this terrible parable.

You need to know that this week's parable is not an isolated story. Last week, you might recall, we lamented the parable of the wicked tenants in the vineyard and the violent attacks they executed. And the week before, it was the parable about people like prostitutes and tax collectors who will get into heaven before people who followed all the rules all their lives. Three weeks ago, I preached on the parable of the workers in yet another vineyard who received the same reward whether they worked twelve hours or one. Do you see a trend here? Is God a God of mercy, or a God of justice? Is he a God of tenderness, or a God of violence? And Matthew's answer seems to be, *yes*. God is a loving God with a harsh side. And this parable of the wedding feast puts that sort of God on display.

In the first part of this parable, the king gives the people a gracious invitation. They didn't earn a seat at the banquet table; they did nothing to deserve it, but the king invited them anyway. When they say "no thank you" the king invites them again. When they turn down the second invite, they probably assumed the king would return a third time, and a fourth, and a fifth. But you cannot reject a king indefinitely, for one day the king's patience will run thin, and there will be no more chances.

Time after time, we take God's grace for granted, don't we? Day after day, we are invited to find shelter in his forgiveness, but we turn him down, because the world offers more excitement than a boring God. Perhaps when we are old and feeble, and have tasted every temptation that the world can give, maybe then we can become serious about our faith. But what if God grows impatient with us? What if there are no more chances? Pastor Frank Harrington said it best, that "The biggest lie the devil tells us is that there will always be more time." Well, maybe there won't be. Have you ever thought about that?

And regarding the wedding guest who refused to put on the robe, perhaps we too refuse to celebrate our place in God's kingdom. We like to feast on God's forgiveness, but we are not willing to accept God's claim upon our lives. The truth is, God accepts us just the way we are, but he is not willing to leave us the way we are. God desires that we grow in obedience to him, and grow in service to our neighbor. I wonder if God becomes weary of my faith talk, when it is not consistent with my faith walk. Because it's not - I'm telling you that today; that my walk and my talk are miles apart. What am I going to do? What are you going to do?

Well, what I'm going to do is tell you that there is another image of God that runs throughout the Bible, and in that image, God is overwhelmingly merciful and kind. Like a parent, this God does become perturbed with his children, but perturbed does not have the final word. Love does. Grace does. Forgiveness is the hallmark of the God we know, and if that's all you remember from this sermon, that that would be enough. Let me close by describing a different sort of party.

Tony Campolo is a sociologist in Philadelphia, and a college professor, and a Baptist evangelist who could easily be Lutheran; I know him that well. Tony was invited to speak at a conference in Hawaii several years ago, and as it so often is when we travel several time zones away, he couldn't sleep, so he walked to an all-night coffee shop at 3 am.[7]

Larry was the cook in that place, a balding man, wearing a grease-stained white T-shirt and smoking a cigarette over the grill. "Whaddya want?" he barked, as Tony sat down. "Just a cup of coffee, and maybe one of those donuts."

As Tony sat there munching on his donut, eight or nine provocative and boisterous prostitutes came into the café and sat at the counter next to him. Tony overheard one of them say to the group, "Tomorrow's my birthday. I'm going to be 39." One of the women said mockingly, "So whaddya want from us, a birthday party! You want us to light candles on a cake and sing happy birthday?"

And the birthday girl said, "Aw, c'mon you guys. Why do you have to be so mean? I was just telling you it's my birthday. I don't want anything from you. I'm 39 years old and I've never had a birthday party in my whole life; why would I start now?"

7 ©1990, Tony Campolo, The Kingdom of God is a Party

When the women left, Tony asked Larry, "Do they come in every night?" Yeah, they do, Larry said. "And the one who was sitting next to me, does she come here every night too?" "Yeah, that's Agnes and she's here every night at 3:30. Why do you want to know?"

And Tony said this; "I heard her say tomorrow is her birthday, and she has never had a birthday party. What do you say we throw her a birthday party right here" A devilish smile spread over Larry's face and he called his wife out from the kitchen and said, "Hey, tomorrow is Agnes' birthday, and this guy thinks we should throw her a party." His wife said, "Oh, Agnes is one of the really nice ones! I'll bake the cake."

At 2:30 the next morning, Tony showed up with crepe paper and balloons, and a sign that read, "Happy Birthday, Agnes!" Apparently, the word got out, because by 3:30 on the dot, the café was wall-to-wall prostitutes. And when Agnes walked in, the crowd broke into a cheer: Happy birthday, Agnes – Happy birthday!

Agnes was flabbergasted. Her mouth fell open, and her legs buckled and one of the girls helped her sit down. When they brought out the cake with candles blazing, and they started to sing, Agnes lost it and she began to weep. "Blow out the candles, Agnes! Blow out the candles!" Agnes didn't know the drill; she had never had a birthday cake before. And then she hesitated, and turned to Larry; "Larry, if it's all right with you, I mean, is it okay if I just take the cake home and keep it for a little while?" When Larry told her it was her cake, Agnes picked up the cake and carefully carried it out of the café. Everyone in the café sat motionless, and then Tony broke the silence by saying, "Why don't we pray?"

Tony would later say that it probably seemed strange that a college professor would lead a prayer meeting with a bunch of prostitutes at 3:30 in the morning. *Ya think?* But he prayed for Agnes, right there in the café. And when he finished that prayer, Harry, the greasy cook, leaned over the counter and said, "Hey, you never told me you were a preacher! What kind of church do you belong to anyway?"

Tony said that the unrehearsed-but-perfect answer came out of his mouth, "I belong to a church that throws birthday parties for whores at 3:30 in the morning." Harry waited a moment, and then he said, "No you don't. There's no church like that. Because if there was, I'd join it. I'd join a church like that!"

People, I believe that Jesus came to create a church like that. His preferred audiences throughout his ministry were not the prim and proper, and filled with the sophisticated people of the world. He came to rub shoulders with the fishermen, the bricklayers, the lepers, and tax collectors, and prostitutes, many of whom the world often ignores. But in the kingdom of God they are not ignored!

Jesus got that parable partly right today. When the king invited the beautiful people to a wedding banquet and they turned him down, God extended his invitation to the homeless, the rejected, and the nobodies of this world. And only when the palace was filled with those grateful people, only then did the party begin. The part he got wrong is that when one of the guests acted inappropriately, the king kicked him out into the darkness.

That's not the God I know. If it were, I don't think I could stand up here and proclaim his love every Sunday. And truthfully, you wouldn't sit there and listen to it.

Because sometimes, we are the ones who do or say the inappropriate thing, and God does not send us out, but draws us closer in. If our church is going to grow in the coming months and years, it will not be because we rejected the very people that Jesus came to save. The church that grows will be the church of open arms, open ears, and open hearts, which invites the people that Jesus loves to hear the powerful message of grace.

We're the servants now, armed with an invitation to a glorious wedding banquet. If we stuff those invitations into our pockets and refuse to share them, our congregation will wither and die. But if we have the courage to invite the outsiders in to join us, this church will become a glorious party of joy. It's our choice. It's our choice. I hope we choose wisely.

Thanks be to God.

Amen.

Trick Questions

Do you like riddles? I've always liked riddles. Riddles are word problems; brilliant questions that stump us, until we are told the answer, and then we can't believe we missed it! Some riddles – especially those we learn in childhood – are rather simple. For example, "What's black and white and read all over?" (A newspaper). Or how about this one, "I am a wealthy doctor, I have a wealthy son. But if you're looking for his father, I am not the one. Who am I?" (His mother).

I recently heard a riddle that was allegedly solved by 80% of kindergarteners, but only 17% of Stanford University students. Here's the riddle:

What is...

More powerful than God

More evil than the devil

Poor people have it

Rich people don't need it

And if you eat it you will die?

And the answer...

Nothing!

In the gospel text that is ours today, the Jewish leaders came to Jesus with a riddle of sorts...a riddle whose answer they are hoping incriminates Jesus. Their initial approach was to suck up to Jesus in order to gain his trust.

"Teacher, we know that you always tell the truth about things…especially when it comes to God, so teacher, we have a question for you. Is it against our religion to pay taxes?"

In a sense, it was a brilliant question. If Jesus said yes, that it was wrong to pay taxes to Caesar, it would place Jesus squarely against the Roman government. Big mistake! But if Jesus said, "pay their taxes" it implied support for the Romans, a people whom the Jews despised. It was a lose/lose situation for Jesus, this brilliant question that the Pharisees had asked him. But then the Pharisees didn't yet know with whom they were dealing!

"Show me one of your coins" Jesus said. "Whose name and face appear on it?"

"Well, that's Caesar's name and face, of course," they said.

"All right then," Jesus answered. "You pay to Caesar that which belongs to Caesar, and you pay to God that which belongs to God. It's that simple!"

From its inception, the church has lived in a tension with government. Our credo, "Jesus is Lord," flies straight into the face of the Roman oath that said, "Caesar is Lord." Early on, Christians drew a line in the sand, confessing, "To God alone we render worship, but in other things we gladly serve you." Certain professions were forbidden for those early believers; for instance: the actor, if he were a Christian, could not play the part of pagan gods, the teacher could not teach pagan mythology, the gladiator could not take human life just for the sport of it. But Christians could pay taxes.

When Jesus offered his brilliant response to the Pharisees, they were amazed; amazed, not because Jesus answered brilliantly, but because he avoided their trap. You see, the Pharisees didn't care about Caesar and taxes. They wanted to embarrass Jesus because he was stirring the pot with all his talk of love and forgiveness and grace. So they kept on asking him trick questions.

Master, we caught this woman in the very act of adultery. Our law says that she should be stoned to death; what do you say? *Which of you has never sinned?*

Master, our law says that no work should be done on the sabbath, so why do you allow your disciples to pick grain on the sabbath? *The sabbath was made for humankind, and not humankind for the sabbath.*

Master, if the greatest commandments are to love God and serve my neighbor, then who, exactly, is my neighbor? *Have you heard the one about the good Samaritan?*

They are all trick questions you see, in an attempt to reduce Jesus' ministry to a bunch of religious rules. But consistently, Jesus insisted that faith is not about rules; rather, it is about a relationship with a loving God. The Pharisees were afraid of Jesus...afraid that he might get to them with his compassion and his tenderness, so they kept Jesus at a distance with their legalistic questions.

In his book *The Screwtape Letters, author* C.S. Lewis described two of the devil's angels. Screwtape is the seasoned veteran, and Wormwood, his nephew, is the novice. Throughout the entire story, they're trying to coax this new Christian away from his faith in God. The wisdom of Screwtape is obvious: "Raise doubts in the man's mind, fill it with questions of reason and rationality," he tells

Wormwood. "Make him ask questions like, 'Why is there war' and 'Why does God permit suffering' and 'What about all the religious hypocrites?'"[8]

In truth, C.S. Lewis is not describing fictional characters in a novel; he describes his former life, and people in our world yet today who want to keep Jesus at arm's length. Like the Pharisees, perhaps they are afraid too, so they ask questions ranging from the ridiculous to the unanswerable; not out of curiosity but out of defense. "If God is all powerful, could he create a rock so big that not even he could lift it?" "How can God send people to hell if they live in Africa and have never heard about him?" "And what about unbaptized babies who die?" Those are not necessarily bad questions, and they should be discussed, but they are questions of the mind. Jesus specialized in questions of the heart. "Do you want to be forgiven?" That was one of his favorites, and it's hard to ponder that question and still remain at a distance.

Many years ago, I met a young woman – I'll call her Amy – who said she had been running from God for several years. She saw the religion of her parents as constraining and prohibitive, so she abandoned it...and them, too. She ran off to Seattle and lived what she said was a very provocative life. She got into drugs, a variety of sexual experiences, and she even dabbled in the occult. But then she got sick; a dirty needle caused infection in her bloodstream, and she was in danger of losing her leg, and all of her newfound friends had left her. Without any other

8 © 1961, C.S. Lewis, *The Screwtape Letters,* Publisher Geoffrey Bles, London England

option, she called her parents, and when her mother answered, she said, "Mom. Can I come home? I think I'm dying."

When Amy flew home, she didn't really know what to expect. Criticism? Condemnation? Interrogation? But when she got off the plane, she was met by the two people in the world who loved her the most. On the way home, they drove to the parking lot of a church; Amy recognized it as the church where they had attended Sunday school fifteen years earlier. "What are we doing here?" Amy impatiently asked.

And her dad began, "Amy, when you were three months old, you were baptized in this church. Two years ago, when you left us, we began coming to this parking lot every Sunday evening and we prayed for you. We prayed that God would keep you safe, and that you would one day find your way back. Today, God has answered our prayers. Welcome home, honey."

I expect there are some Pharisees in worship with us today. Maybe you're new, and you have no clue why you even came here today. Maybe you worship here every Sunday, but you find yourself in a wilderness place now, running away from the God of your childhood. Maybe you are one who has put up all the defenses, asked all the hard questions without finding any answers, and life has remained a riddle. Or perhaps you are an elder Pharisee; you know scripture, you've memorized scripture, but for some reason, the joy has gone. Whatever your circumstance, you're here today to hear the great good news that

Jesus has been your near companion all along. Welcome home, friend. The Savior has brought you home, no questions asked.

Thanks be to God.

Amen.

A Tale Of Two Churches

Dear friends in Christ, grace to you, and peace, from God our Father, and his Son, our Lord and Savior, Jesus Christ. Amen.

I once heard the story of a pastor who was in the final preparations for retirement. He had been serving in his congregation for many years, but he was weary, and the time was right, and in just a few short weeks, he would bid them farewell. Then one night, he had a dream...

He dreamed that though he had resettled in a distant city during retirement, he was visiting the community of that final congregation he had served. As he drove into the lot, the first thing he noticed was the great number of cars; curb to curb, far more cars than he had ever seen in his career there. And when he entered the building, he was greeted with dozens of smiling people whom he had never met before; "new members" he surmised. He found a seat as the music began, and the music was grand. Then the wine arrived, and he assumed they were beginning worship with Holy Communion; "That's creative!" he thought. The pastor leaned over to his seatmate and said, "Is it always this crowded at this service?"

The gentleman smiled warmly and said, "Oh, this isn't a church anymore. Apparently, when the pastor left several years ago, the membership declined and the church closed, so a young couple bought it and turned it into a jazz nightclub; don't you love it?"

The pastor awoke in a cold sweat and remembered clearly the dream he had. He loved that congregation so much, and while his ministry had been meaningful and deep, he suddenly realized that he had done little to prepare the church for the future. Where would they go, what would they do, what kind of church would they be in the future? And early on that Tuesday morning, he called the congregational president and said that he was delaying his retirement for two years, because he had work to do!

You may have noticed that two gospel texts were read today, both from Matthew's gospel. This wasn't a typo or an accident; rather, it was an intentional effort to look at two churches that Matthew imagined.

The first of the two lessons is commonly known to us as The Great Commandment. A Pharisee approached Jesus one day and asked him yet another trick question: This is almost a do-over of last week's text, when the Pharisees are again trying to paint Jesus into a corner. So this week, Jesus was asked, "Master, which commandment is the greatest?" Moses gave the Jews Ten Commandments from God, but the Jews also had more than 600 other laws by which they were required to live. And here's the "trick" part of the question: If Jesus identified one commandment as the greatest; he would have been accused of overlooking hundreds of other laws the Jews followed. As always, Jesus was brilliant! He answered, "*You shall love God with all your heart and soul and mind and strength.* That's the first. But the second is just like it; *You shall love your neighbor as yourself.* Upon these two commandments all of the laws and all of the words of the prophets are dependent."

Even if you listened to those two commands carefully, you still might have missed the only common word in both of them; it's a verb, and it's the word "love." Love God. Love your neighbor. Simple as that! Before the Pharisee can even begin to criticize Jesus for his answer, Jesus was announcing that the kingdom of God was not to be built on rules! The kingdom is built upon relationships. Love God! Love your neighbor. Everything else in life will be in harmony if you can master those two relationships.

Six chapters later, Jesus offered his disciples what we have come to know as The Great Commission. First, The Great Commandment, and now, The Great Commission. After Jesus had been nailed to the cross, and after he had risen from the grave, but just before he ascended into heaven, Jesus left his remaining eleven disciples with a parting word, and this is what he said. "Go to all the world and make disciples, baptize them in the name of the Father, Son, and Holy Spirit. Teach them to obey everything I have commanded you. And remember that I will always be with you." In this directive, Jesus uses four verbs. Holy cow, four verbs in a single sentence, and here are the words; "Go, make disciples, baptize, and teach."

In other words, leave the comfort of your sanctuary and "Go" into the world armed with the good news of the gospel. "Tell" them the story of the cross; "Mark them" as part of the community of the forgiven, and "Teach them" to obey the expectations of the Lord. Verbs are action words, and perhaps these verbs should be followed by exclamation points. Go! Tell! Mark them! Teach them! Just do it! That's the Great Commission.

Over my ministry, I have noticed that some churches are Great Commandment churches. They exude love. They express their love for God in worship; they show their love for their church family, and their neighbors. They hug visitors and invite them to gather for coffee and cookies after worship. They bring meals to the homebound. Great Commandment churches reach out to the hungry, and the hurting, and the persecuted. They build homes with Habitat for Humanity, they pray without ceasing for those who are in need. They excel at loving God and caring for their neighbor, whoever their neighbor may be.

But often times, these same churches are not very good at going into the world and making disciples. And as a Lutheran, I can say this: some of these are Lutheran churches. I mean, shoveling someone's sidewalk comes easily for us, but talking about our faith is the harder thing. So we are reluctant to tell people about Jesus, we're not comfortable teaching them the Bible, and even inviting them to church might be out of our comfort zone. I mentioned in a sermon years ago, a statistic that said Lutherans invite people to come to their church once every 56 years! (I know, right?). The next week, Chuck Lawson came up to me after worship, and introduced me to two friends and said, "I've done my job for the next 112 years!" That's a Great Commandment church.

Great Commission churches are *always* talking about Jesus. They wear their faith on their sleeve, or on their car bumpers. They study their bibles and they gather others to do so as well. They have training in how to lead people to Christ; they send people on mission trips, not to build Habitat houses, but to share the gospel with those who will live in the Habitat houses. One young member of a Great Commission church was asked what his purpose in life was, and without skipping a beat said, "My purpose in life is to go to heaven and take as many people as I can with me!" So they warn people of what the future holds if they don't believe in Jesus, and they explain plainly and clearly what it means to be a disciple of Jesus Christ. With warm smiles and great enthusiasm, the members of Great Commission churches do evangelism very, very well.

Over my ministry, I have noticed that what they don't do all that well is to love the people they are reaching out to. If those people don't follow the rules that Jesus taught, or if they start following, and then fall off the wagon, it seems like the evangelists are disappointed in them. Then they become busy finding new people to evangelize, and teach the rules to.

So, here's the question: Is our church a Great Commandment church, or are we a Great Commission church? And before you answer that question in your head, let me stop you.

The church of Jesus Christ is the one that exhibits both. It is a congregation that is filled with love for God, and love for all the people that God loves. It's a church that shows Christ by acts of kindness, charity, and compassion. But the church of Jesus Christ is also a congregation that boldly tells the story of Jesus to those who have never heard it. Members of the church of Jesus unapologetically admit that they are sinners who have been forgiven, and their purpose in life is to speak and live the gospel, so that people will be drawn to Jesus and his church. Jesus did not create two churches; he created *one church* that would love and serve, and teach and tell; and a church like that could change the world.

That story I told you at the outset of this sermon, about the pastor that had the dream…someone told me that story years ago, and I don't even know if it's true. But I don't want that story to be true in this church. We have work to do here; we have plans to make, and leaders to choose, and budgets to adopt, and children to teach, and strangers to welcome. That's why we were planted here so many years ago, and it is still our reason for being.

When I visited Independence Hall in Philadelphia, the tour guide told the story of the chair that the speaker of the legislature had been sitting in during the Continental Congress. It was a wooden high back chair that had a sun etched into the front of it. When the Declaration of Independence had been signed, Benjamin Franklin arose and said, "All these days I have been looking at the speaker's chair, wondering if that was a setting sun or a rising sun. I am glad to say today that it is surely a rising sun." After 164 years of ministry in this congregation, I want to share the attitude of Franklin: that the sun is just rising on us, and we have work to do.

Thanks be to God.

Amen.

Proper 26 / Ordinary Time 31
Matthew 23:1-12

(Don't) Follow Me

Dear friends in Christ, grace to you, and peace, from God our Father, and his Son, our Lord and Savior, Jesus Christ. Amen.

It's been a hard season for leaders; leaders of every stripe, strata, and profession. In 2017, a wave of allegations of sexual impropriety swept across our nation. The epicenter of what came to be known as *#metoo movement*, was Hollywood, but nearly every corner of our culture has been indicted. Women (but men, too!) would no longer be silent about the conduct of abusers, attackers, bullies and serial creeps. And the movement resulted in a tsunami of cultural change about how our nation relates to power. Because that's what is at the core of *#me too*: not sex, not job termination or political agendas - power. And just so you know it, it's not a new thing.

In our gospel lesson today, Jesus had just finished telling a string of parable to his disciples, but also to a swelling crowd, and the common thread of the stories was power; exerting it, threatening it, and abusing it. And it led Jesus to point the finger at his religious adversaries, the Pharisees.

Do you know the Pharisees; these men of first century Judaism who insisted upon strict observance of Jewish Law? Their reputation was superior piety, which distinguished them above all other Jews. Even their name gives them away: "Pharisees; men who separated themselves." They would freely call out the sins of the common folk, wag their fingers at them and shame them into repentance. The most radical among them would wear blinders on the sides of their heads to shield their eyes from having to see these sinners; however this led to their bumping into lampposts and buildings, thus, the label, *those bleeding Pharisees!"*

They determined how the law ought to be observed, but also, how it might be avoided. They even crafted escape clauses that enabled them to do work on the sabbath. Listen to the words that were written by these religious leaders of the day:

To carry *anything* on the sabbath is forbidden. He who carries anything, whether it be in his right hand, or his left hand, or in his bosom, or on his shoulder is guilty. But he who carries anything on the back of his hand, or with his foot, or with his mouth, or with his elbow; or with his ear, or with his hair, or with his money bag and his shirt, or in the fold of his shirt, or in his shoe, or in his sandal is not guilty because he does not carry it in the usual way of carrying it.

This is how the scribes and the Pharisees observed and avoided the law. Then they condemned anyone who did not do it their way. And all of this was done in the name of religion.

All of this is in the windshield of Jesus in today's gospel lesson:

Do whatever they teach you and follow it; but do not do as they do, for they do not practice what they teach.

They tie up heavy burdens, hard to bear, and lay them on the shoulders of others; but they themselves are unwilling to lift a finger to move them.

They love to have the place of honor at banquets and the best seats in the synagogues, and to be greeted with respect in the marketplaces, and to have people call them rabbi.

Do you see the hypocrisy in the Pharisees' lives? They remind me of the idiom of a salmon fisherman I met in Oregon, describing believers who do not walk their talk. "They are the mackerel in the moonlight" he said, "they look good but they stink!" Jesus thought so too. He was not condemning them for their practice of calling people to righteous living; he was condemning the Pharisees for their own practice of unrighteousness. And here is the irony of Jesus' words, according to Alyce Mckenzie:

"The listeners of Jesus' day would have expected the Pharisee to be a careful observer of the Law. They would not have expected the tax collector to go to the temple at all."[9]

No wonder Jesus was so hard on the Pharisees! They criticized Jesus and his disciples for the way they did not wash their hands, and the way they snacked on the heads of grain on the sabbath, while they themselves lived their sinful lives in secret. At one point in Luke's gospel, Jesus would again chastise them; "woe to you Pharisees" he

9 © 2011 Alyce Mckenzie, www.patheos.com

would say, followed by a litany of their faults. I, for one, am glad that I don't serve in a religious culture that is led by Pharisees. But, maybe I do!

As difficult as these remaining moments of this sermon will be for me, I need to confess that I am more like the Pharisees than I even want to admit. And not me alone, but many – perhaps most – of my sisters and brothers who serve as pastors in the twenty-first century church. We preach a good game; we may offer spellbinding descriptions of how the Savior has called us to live our lives, in spite of the fact that we live in a state of grace. We stand up on Sunday mornings and call our flocks to paths of humble faith and righteous living. Then we go home and defy our own words. Our sin is not our actions alone, but our inactions as well. Our sins include dishonesty when we stand in this holy place and present ourselves as holier than you. People, we have met the Pharisees and they are us.

It used to be that when pastors made the news, it was because of a momentous gathering, or a new ministry initiative, or a column of encouragement or guidance. These days, clergy are the news, and for far more scandalous reasons. The failures of Jim Bakker, Jimmy Swaggart, and Ted Haggard were well documented in the late twentieth century. More recently, the plethora of child sexual abuse among priests, the plagiarisms by some, the indiscretions by others, and the opulent lifestyles of more than a few clergy; these shock us and wound the whole church.

But as pastors – like the Pharisees – we are not fooling anyone. You know we are human. You know that our list of imperfections can match yours any day. A recent poll by the Gallup Organization identified the professions that are most and least respected in America.[10] Let's do a little crowd participation: What occupations do you think lead the list of most and least respected in America today *(invite congregation to call out their responses)*. Gallup's list of honesty and ethics in professions may surprise you:

Nurses	82%
Military officers	71%
Elementary School teachers	66%
(good for you, teachers!)	
Medical doctors	65%
Pharmacists	62%
Police officers	56%
Daycare providers	46%
Judges	43%

Are you wondering when the clergy are going to show up? We come in at 42%; just barely above auto mechanics, lawyers, car salespeople, and members of congress. Don't you wonder how Jesus would have responded if he had been asked to fill out this survey?

All of this is to say that talk is cheap, the Savior has called us to honesty and action; and that goes for bricklayers, police officers, sales clerks, presidents, Pharisees, and pastors. To walk the talk of Jesus is to serve as his hands and feet and lips in a hurting world. I can't speak for all pastors today, but I can speak for this one: forgive me for my hypocrisy, and I will forgive you for yours.

Thanks be to God.

Amen.

10 © 2017, The Gallup Organization, as reprinted in *Forbes Magazine*

All Saints' Sunday
Matthew 5:1-12

Giving Back

Dear friends in Christ, grace to you, and peace, from God our Father, and his Son, our Lord and Savior, Jesus Christ. Amen.

For the first thirty years of my life, All Saints' Sunday didn't mean much to me. In fact, for the first thirty years, I didn't even know what it was. I didn't know it was a day in the year of the church when we lift up the names of those we love who have entered the kingdom of heaven. I wasn't pastor yet, but the year that I turned 32, my grandfather died and I did the funeral. That's the year I learned about All Saints' Day; when they read the names of the saints of that congregation, and I whispered the name of my grandfather. He was kind of gruff, kind of rough around the edges, but he loved me, that much I knew. And I am reminded of something Mr. Rogers once sang:[11]

Even people who are good most of the time are bad some of the time.

And people who are bad most of the time are good some of the time.

---

11 Lyrics by Fred Rogers provided courtesy of The Fred Rogers Company.

That's who the Saints are; people who were not perfect, people who were good some of the time, and not so
good some of the time, but they were people who touche
our lives and left us a legacy to follow. And that's why we
speak their names today,

And I wonder if, a generation from now, the church
will celebrate All Saints' Sunday. What will we say we
left them, aside from trillion dollar debts, and a wounded
planet? But I know what my grandfather's generation left
me...left us. And these Beatitudes that Jesus described in
the gospel today become sort of a checklist of the greatest
generation's legacy. Because though they were poor, they
gave anyway. When they mourned, they leaned on God
and each other. When they were hungry, they didn't have
community food shelves; they were the community and
they ate together. They showed mercy and they received
mercy. They fought wars because they sought peace, not
because they sought domination, or oil. And they left us a
spirit of hope, and faith in a God that will always be present with us, no matter what.

A man had taken his grandson to visit an historic
church, which displayed ancient stained glass windows
picturing biblical stories. As they walked around the nave,
the little boy pointed at one of the bright windows and
asked, "Who are those people, Grandpa?" And grandpa
said, "Those are the saints." "Oh, I get it; saints are people
who let the light shine through!"

I mention all of this today, not to be all melancholy and
nostalgic, but to gently challenge the saints of this generation; our generation. People, we have been blessed.
Yes, these recent years have been difficult, but every age

has difficult times. Yes, the culture has changed; we are more divided than at any time since the Civil War, and the Christian church is more divided than it was a generation ago. The makeup of families has changed. The nature of our neighborhoods has changed; in many cases, we don't even know our neighbors. Our respect for our leaders and authorities has changed. Everything has changed: But the promises of God have not changed. Nor will they ever changed. How does Hebrews say it? "Jesus Christ is the same; yesterday, today, and forever."

So how do we live as saints in a changing world? If we're not going back to the 1950s – and here is breaking news: we're not going back to the 1950s – so in light of this, how do we walk as saints in a 2020 world?

The place to begin is to trust God at his word; to believe the promises of God. Someone once actually searched the Bible and counted how many there are. Who has the time to do that, but someone did, and found 3573 promises in scripture. Do you know any of them? Can you recite any promises God has made to you? How about:

I have called you by name, you are mine.

As far as the east is from the west, so far has he removed our sins from us.

For God so loved the world that he gave his only Son, so that whoever believes in him will have eternal life.

I am with you always, even to the end of time.

As we begin to learn these promises and internalize them, we come to realize that we are special to God. That is not to say, as some of our more righteous friends are wont to say that, "God is on our side." That kind of arrogance is why the church is so divided in our world. But to know that we are special in God's eyes, that God laughs when we laugh, and God weeps when we weep; that God walks with us in this crazy, changing world. Do you believe that? Do you believe that God walks with you? Because if you do, if I do, then it changes the way we live our lives. It changes how we read those words of Jesus in the gospel today.

Suddenly the word "blessed" may not mean a comfortable home, or a conflict-free family, or giant bank accounts, or perfect health. For the saints, being blessed means that the circumstances of our lives do not change God's plan for us. Everybody mourns; everybody goes through periods of discouragement, and everybody experiences times of feeling picked on and persecuted. What Jesus was saying in this Sermon on the Mount was ,"Look, following me will not insulate you from the problems of life, but it will give you the courage to endure the storms, because I have a home for you in the kingdom. I have forgiveness for you for all the times you have messed up. I have a community to surround you, and a joy that sustains you, and a promise that tells you your future is secure." These words of Jesus are not simply to pacify us, or to draw us into delusional thinking. They are truths from the mouth of God.

And as people who profess those truths, we know that our future is secure. We trust God's promise that he knows us intimately and follows us all of our days, we don't have to chase the security that the world offers. We are free to live, and to love, and to share, and to be a friend to others.

And that's it. That's the ultimate purpose of the saints, a hundred years ago, two millennia ago, and yet today: that we are called to live, love, share, and reach out in friendship. It doesn't mean we live like paupers, nor does it mean that we artificially act as if problems don't concern us. After all;

Even people who are good most of the time are bad some of the time. And people who are bad most of the time are good some of the time.

That's us, right? Because we are the saints.

It means that we read the last chapter of the mystery novel first and we know how it ends. Do you ever do that? Sneak a peek at the final paragraph and see who's still alive? That's how it is for us. We know that in the final paragraph, the saints will be living in a glorious place, and we will join them there. So until then, we emulate the saints who lived among us; those who gave their time, and shared their possessions, and dreamed dreams and fulfilled them, and left them all for us. May we do the same until our journey ends.

Thanks be to God.

Amen.

Burning The Midnight Oil

Dear friends in Christ, grace to you, and peace, from God our Father, and his Son, our Lord and Savior, Jesus Christ. Amen.

It has been several decades since Pastor John Lloyd Ogilvie wrote his book about the parables of Jesus titled, *The Autobiography of God.* As Ogilvie pointed out, this "autobiography" – this self-writing – is exactly what the parables of Jesus are.[12] They are the description of the kingdom of God by God's own self." Jesus did not write them down as an author would; he told them to small groups, to angry crowds, to the masses, to individuals, and most often, to his disciples. He painted word-pictures about what life would be like on the other side. And all of these centuries later, Christians young and old have continued to gain glimpses of heaven by reading and telling the stories Jesus told.

We learn from God's autobiography that the kingdom of heaven is not at all like the kingdom of the world. There are differences; significant differences. Differences that affect how we look at life in God's kingdom on earth. For instance, in God's kingdom, fathers forgive sons, even though the sons may thoughtlessly squander half of the

12 © 1981, The Autobiography of God, John Lloyd Ogilvie, Baker Publishing

family fortune. In the kingdom of heaven, workers who work one hour are paid the same as the workers who worked a lifetime. In the kingdom, going out of one's way for one's neighbor is honored and encouraged, and self-serving security is despised. In the kingdom of God, a shepherd will leave 99 sheep in the pasture in order to seek the one who had wandered away. These are the parables. This is God's autobiography.

And yet, we read these stories and scratch our heads at their crazy implications – and they are crazy, you know! – we wonder about their practicality. Prodigal sons and good Samaritans are not of much value in the world's twenty-first-century economy. Looking for one lost lamb is not a cost-effective practice. Labor unions will not allow a full day's pay for a half-day of work unless everybody gets it. In short, the parables that describe the kingdom are very different from the world in which you and I live. But you already knew that.

Yet, the parable that stands before us today is unique. This is one that we could have written, for there is much similarity between the parable and our contemporary world. In Jesus' parable, people who are not prepared are called "foolish." We would concur. "Get your own oil, I'm not sharing!" Those are our words precisely. "You were too late; you can't come in." Spoken like one of us. This is a parable with our own world's values intact, and yet Jesus says that this, too, is how it will be in the kingdom of heaven. This is a parable of watching and waiting and being ready. If it sounds too harsh to come from Jesus' lips, then perhaps we have misunderstood the parable. There's got to be a word of grace here, right? There simply has to be, for this is the autobiography of God, for heaven's sake!

On the front chancel wall at Our Savior's Lutheran Church in Sioux Falls, South Dakota, there is a forty-foot high mural depicting the ascension of Jesus. All of the disciples are present there, along with Mary, and Mary Magdalene, and two brightly-dressed angels. The words written at the bottom of the mural are attributed to those angels:

"Galileans, why do you stand looking up into heaven? This same Jesus whom you saw go up into heaven will come again in the same way."

So the waiting had officially begun. Anyone who knew of Jesus recounted the times he had promised that he would return, and the angels of Ascension Day confirmed it. But you see, most thought Jesus' return was imminent. It would only be a matter of a few days…a couple of weeks at most. And so these faithful Christian people waited… and waited…and waited for the return of the Savior.

Have you ever waited for someone who was late? Sure you have. A Friday night date, or a ride to work, or dinner guests? It's the most exasperating thing we ever do – to wait. When they're just a few minutes late, we're relieved because we really weren't ready for them anyway! When they are half an hour late, we get angry. After an hour, we become worried. But sooner or later in our waiting, we think the dreaded thought. "I'll bet they aren't coming at all. No phone call. No email. They're simply not going to show."

The ascension of Jesus took place in 29 AD, Matthew's gospel was written about 70 AD. By the time Matthew had recorded this parable, the Christian Church had already waited for more than forty years. Do you suppose that waiting got pretty old after forty years? Do you suppose some Christians lost interest or patience, or even lost faith that Jesus would ever come back for them? I mean, how much oil do you need in your lamp to keep it burning for forty years?

But it has now been two millennia since the ascension of Jesus, and the idea that the Christian church is waiting in breathless anticipation for him to return has grown pretty dim. We say we are waiting…watching…anticipating, but in the meantime, other things have captured our attention. We're raising our children. We're planning for our retirements. We're arranging 30-year mortgages on our homes. And all of this is done without much thought to the coming of Christ. I mean, he didn't come last century. He hasn't come so far this century. Who knows? He might not be coming at all.

But you see, he is coming; scripture promises it. We don't know when; Jesus indicated that he didn't even know when. Not even those angels in heaven know when. But I can tell you that today, and the gospel readings in Advent will reinforce the promise, that Jesus is indeed coming again.

So in the meantime, what do we do? We sleep. Like the maidens in our parable, we sleep during this wait that seems endless. And that's okay. Notice that the maidens in the story were not criticized for their slumber. And notice too, that both maidens wise and maidens foolish were able to sleep, though I think for different reasons. The foolish maidens slept out of boredom. They had long since lost interest in ever seeing the bridegroom, and their lack of oil was an indication of their apathy. They never really expected to see the bridegroom. The wise maidens, however, were able to sleep because they were at peace. Their oil lamps were full. They had done all they could in preparation. They were ready, with nothing left to do but wait.

This parable of the maidens, if it does anything, it encourages us to keep our oil lamps filled as we wait. The oil is not our good deeds. It is not doing things that will make Jesus love us more. The oil is not jumping through hoops until Jesus comes, so that when he does come, he will be impressed with our effort. We have grace for that! The oil of our lamps is the oil of faith. It is the oil of prayer. It is the oil of loving Jesus and serving our neighbor. Our oil is replenished through the study of God's word, and singing hymns of praise, and recalling the depth of his love. Being ready is not being perfect. Being ready might not even mean being awake. Being ready is trusting that God's promises are true, and God's grace is sufficient.

Many years ago, I saw a young man at the state fair wearing a T-shirt with the likeness of Jesus on the front, and these words printed there:

Jesus is coming soon…

And as he walked by, I noticed that the back of the shirt completed the message:

And is he ticked off!

People, he is coming soon, and he comes in judgment, but he is not ticked off. He comes in love, and compassion; filled with grace. He comes looking for the flames that flicker in the lives of those who wait.

Thanks be to God.

Amen.

Investment Choices

Dear friends in Christ, grace to you and peace, from God our Father, and his Son, our Lord and Savior, Jesus Christ. Amen.

I started reading crime novels about fifteen years ago. Like any pastor, so much of what I read relates to theology or ministry that I needed to find some genre of reading that would take me away from what I do twelve hours a day; something to capture my imagination. I started with John Grisham and read everything he has written. Then I moved on to Swedish author Henning Mankell and read all of his stuff. More recently, I have been reading the murder mysteries of Lee Childs. There is nothing like a good "whodunit" to take my weary brain away from council meetings and budget conversations.

I mention this to you this morning because of a quote I recently came across from Ray Stedman. He wrote:

Parables can be as exciting and challenging as detective stories. But parables, like detective stories, are filled with half-hidden truths and secret meanings and clues to these secrets. Parables are God's exciting way of challenging us to a mystery hunt, and the treasure we are after is a new insight into the nature of life which will enrich us in a thousand ways if we act upon it once it is discovered.[13]

13 © 1970 Living Dangerously, www.raystedman.org

A parable is a mystery, with clues that lead to learning a secret; I had never thought of the parables of Jesus that way. But today, just such a mystery stands before us, and Jesus is daring us to investigate what it might mean to our lives.

A man is going on a journey, but before he does, he leaves some of his possessions – *his* possessions – with three employees. To one he left five talents, to another two talents, and to a third, one talent. If we assume in this contemporary age that the man left talents – like singing, or bricklaying, or slalom skiing – then we will never grasp the mystery. But if we realize that in the time of Jesus, a talent was a weight of measure, like an ounce or a pound, *that* changes everything. So how about if we say it this way; a man left one employee five pounds of gold, and to another he left two pounds of gold, and to the third, he left a pound of gold - serious money - serious responsibility. And he left the various sums based on what each employee's ability was to handle such responsibility.

Then the man returned, he called each employee in to account for what was done with the boss's wealth. The five pounds of gold guy doubled his money, and the boss was pleased. The two pound guy did the same. But the servant with one pound merely brought back the boss's gold; didn't gain any, didn't lose any, because he buried it for safekeeping. The owner called the servant "wicked" and lazy" and he took the gold away from that servant and gave it to the others. Like most investors, the owner didn't just want the return *of* his investment, he also wanted a return *on* his investment, and the third servant failed him.

Now I know what you're thinking; you're thinking, what if you had left your pension fund or your retirement savings with the third servant during the last recession, but instead, you entrusted your accumulated wealth to professionals. Who knew that burying our cash would have been brilliant? I actually know a man who, in the summer of 2008, inherited a great sum of money when his father died. He put it in the local bank because he was too busy to meet with his financial planner. Over the ensuing months, he would have lost 25% of it, but he was ecstatic to simply keep the principle. But sooner or later, he's got to put that money somewhere; to make it grow, to make it work for him. That's what the owner in this parable had intended to do.

So what do you make of this parable that Jesus told? Nice story? Surprise ending, just like in a murder mystery? Or was there something that Jesus would have us learn from this parable that will, as Ray Stedman suggests, "enrich us in a thousand different ways, once we discover its meaning"?

Then consider this; that the parable actually has to do with the blessings that have been given to us by God in this life. Did I say "given?" I meant loaned. Like the owner going on the journey, God has loaned to us these vast gifts; both financial and personal. It's a clue in this mystery of living that many fail to see, or choose to ignore; that the stuff, and the talents and the abilities we possess aren't really our own doing. They don't belong to us, we just think they do. We think we were born poor and worked ourselves rich, or that we were born dumb and worked ourselves smart. And therefore, everything we have is earned and deserved. But that's not what the parable says; the parable says they belong to the master.

So the ultimate meaning of this parable can only be found when we ask this question: What does God want us to do with the blessings that he has loaned to us? And what will happen to us if we fail to do it? It's not a simple question, and we must not take it lightly. Because God cares how we answer it. And this is what I believe God is *not* calling us to do with his wealth. I don't think he would have us spend it all on ourselves and those in our family. I don't think God would have us buy more stuff, travel to more places, treat ourselves to more luxuries, and build up for ourselves more security. Yes, of course God calls us to provide for the needs of those we love; we are not commanded to be peasants. But I *do* believe that God wants a return on his investment, and the return he is looking for is the expanding of the kingdom of God. To quote a question that my friend Tom Nyman loves to ask: "What have you done for God lately?"

Have you shared a portion of your prosperity with the Valley Outreach so that they might provide for those who are without? Have you made a gift to the United Way? Did you fill a Thanksgiving bag for the Union Gospel Mission? Are your kids packing a box for Operation Christmas Child? You see, all of this expands the kingdom of God. By feeding the hungry and clothing the naked and visiting the sick and the imprisoned…by giving anything to a neighbor, we are giving it to God.

I want to speak about giving to our congregation. Your response to our needs this year has been nothing less than astonishing. We've paid all our bills, we've met all our needs. In addition, we've given away nearly $100,000 to ministry partners like Valley Outreach and Young Life. All of this becomes evidence that we are expanding the kingdom of God. In a year of scarcity and challenge, this congregation has been the five bags of gold servant, and I thank you for your generosity.

In the coming year, the needs will be greater. Our ministry costs will be higher. If we fail to meet the worship needs of this body of Christ, or if we fail to teach every child in our midst about the Savior, or if we fail to share with those who are without, then we become the one pound of gold congregation. And why? Because there are enough resources among the members and friends of this church to meet and exceed our budget. And only when we bury what we have been given, or spend it selfishly or foolishly; only then do we fail to return to God what is rightfully his.

And now, allow me to provide a worthy investment opportunity. Next week you will receive a letter and an "Intent of Giving" card, and you'll be asked to return it next Sunday. And today, I am asking you not to bury it. Please don't toss it in the recycle bin, or set aside with the comment "We don't pledge." I am asking you to pray about it, to talk to your family about it, to reflect on what it is you love about this church; and then decide what part of your resources God is calling you to commit. You have investment choices to make. Make them wisely. Make them joyfully. Make them count for the kingdom of God.

Thanks be to God.

Amen.

Reign of Christ / Christ The King Sunday / Ordinary Time 34
Matthew 25:31-46

Going And Doing

Dear friends in Christ, grace to you and peace, from God our Father, and his Son, our Lord and Savior, Jesus Christ. Amen.

Today is the end of the church year. The school year ends in June, and the calendar year ends on December 31, but the church year ends always on a Sunday in late November, and the new church year begins with the season of Advent. Next week, I'll begin a sermon series called START HERE; appropriate for a new year, with a blank canvas standing before us. But as we today focus on the Reign of Christ, it also seemed like a good time to give you a prologue of where it all started. That's what the START HERE series will focus upon.

I begin today asking us to consider where faith started for us. In truth, it started at the beginning of time, and when the Word became flesh and dwelt among us. That's what John's gospel tells us. The start continued on the day that some pastor, somewhere, sprinkled water on our foreheads and marked us with God's promise. And perhaps faith started to become real for us when a loved one said to us "come and see, come and hear, about this man named Jesus."

If we think long enough and hard enough, it seems like our faith is all about us. That Jesus came to bring us promise and purpose and peace and joy, and I suppose in that regard, it is all about us. But the moment we come to the realization that we are sons and daughters of the king…it's not about us anymore. It's about others. The church was never intended to be a closed circle where we sit around, singing "Kum Ba Yah," and care only for ourselves. The church has always been about others. About one hundred fifty years ago, a young minister by the name of William Booth was captured by a passion for the lost and poorest in London, England. The organization he formed is known to us today as The Salvation Army. When Booth died at the age of 83, surrounded by his family, that last word that he spoke was "others." One word - others.

In our gospel lesson today, Jesus is speaking privately with his and he tells them this parable;

"Imagine the king of heaven, sitting on the throne, surrounded by all the nations of the world, and he separates them; some on the left and some on the right. To those on the right he says 'When I was hungry, you fed me. I was thirsty and you gave me something to drink. I was naked and you clothed me. I was sick, and imprisoned and you visited me.' And the people were shocked! 'Lord, when did we feed you, or clothe you, or visit you?' And Jesus said 'Whenever you did it to one of the least, you did it to me.'"

It's important to note that Jesus does not say, "You fed thousands. You clothed millions. You visited throngs of needy people." What he said was whenever you did it for *one of the lowly ones*, you did it for me.

Jesus continues the parable by turning to those on his left; 'When I was hungry, or thirsty, or naked, or imprisoned, or sick, you did nothing for me.' And the people on the left were astonished! 'Lord, when? If we had known that it was you, we'd have fed you a banquet! If we had recognized you, we'd have given you our own coats. If only we had known it was you who was sick, we would have come and prayed for you.' Then Jesus said *'If you refused to do it for others...then you refused to do it for me.'"*

I taught this lesson at a Wednesday morning Bible study and we had a hearty discussion about it. And I had about six meetings that day, so I headed on my way, but first I decided to grab a quick hamburger at McDonalds, and when I walked in, I saw this scraggly, unkempt man sitting alone in a booth, sipping his coffee. The only empty seat that noon was about three booths away, so when I ate my lunch, I overheard him ask a man near him if he could give him a ride to Target. "No" was the answer that quickly came out of his mouth. Next, he asked a passerby for a ride to Target, but the man explained that the cab of his pickup truck was filled with stuff and there was no room. He yelled over his shoulder to two women sitting across the aisle, "Will you drive me to Target?" "We're not planning to leave McDonalds for an hour or more" they said.

And then I began to pray for the man. But here was my prayer; "Lord, please don't let the man ask me to take him to Target. I'm in a hurry, and he's drunk, and I don't want to get involved, so please Lord, don't let him ask..." And my prayer was interrupted by a voice; "Hey brother" the man said, "can you give me a ride to Target?" "Umm, yes, I could do that."

As he arose, he was so unsteady on his feet that I offered my arm, and as we went through the first set of
doors, he fell flat on his face. The McDonald's staff rushed
over as the man spewed a string of four-letter words. One
of the kids from McDonalds suggested that he sit back
down and have another cup of coffee. "Yeah, that's a good
idea" I said, and I left him and walked out to my car. But I
couldn't leave. So I went back in and helped him into my
car and we drove toward Target. "You a doctor or a law-
yer or something?" he asked. "No, I'm not one of those," I
said, rather sheepishly.

He told me his name was Andy, and he used to drive
garbage truck, but he broke his kneecap and he couldn't
drive, and he couldn't afford a doctor, so it self-healed, but
he was always in pain. He asked me if I had any money to
give to him, and I happened to have $5 in my pocket so I
gave him that. Again, with a string of four-letter words, he
said that he had nothing, he didn't have a blanking thing,
and blanking this, and blanking that. "And now" he said,
"I've left my blanking gloves at McDonalds." So I handed
him my gloves.

When we got to Target, I helped him out of the car and
his own gloves fell from his lap to the pavement. "Hey
Andy, you didn't lose your gloves; look, they're right
here." And he said "Okay, you take those and I'll keep
yours!" But I said, "You know, yours are all broken for
your hands, so let's just keep our own, okay?"

When we got inside, he sat on a bench and I shook his
hand and said "God bless you, Andy." And he responded, "He already has brother. He already has." I don't tell
you that story to lift myself up; good grief, I tried twice to

avoid Andy altogether. I tell you that story for the same reason Jesus told his parable; to remind us of others, all around us there are others who have needs that we can fill. And what if the Andy's in our midst *are* Jesus?

In the coming weeks, we will begin preparing the budget for coming year. We will plug in a whole gob of money to pay our staff, money for our programs, purchase Bibles for our kids, send our teenagers to camp, and provide donuts and coffee for our Sunday morning fellowship. Lots of our $1.6 million budget will be spent to serve ourselves… but I wonder how much will be budgeted to serve others? It will not be a measure of our faith, or of our knowledge of scripture, or of our faithfulness in worship; it will be a measure of our mercy, and Jesus said that mercy is what will separate the sheep from the goats. It will be a measure of going and doing for others.

At the end of one church year, and a week before a sermon series titled START HERE, perhaps our serving is best defined by the words of John Wesley;

"Do all the good you can. By all the means you can.
In all the ways you can. In all the places you can.
At all the times you can. To all the people you can.
As long as ever you can."
Because Andy is waiting for us.
Thanks be to God.
Amen.

Thanksgiving
Luke 17:11-19

The Ten-Percenters

Dear friends in Christ, grace to you, and peace, from God our Father, and his Son, our Lord and Savior, Jesus Christ. Amen.

Pastor Virgil Johnson was a soldier. Long before he wore a red clergy stole, presided at weddings, preached Sunday morning sermons, and visited the sick; back when he was a very young man, Virgil wore green camoglage and was a private in the United States Army, stationed somewhere in Europe near the end of World War Two. In the early spring of 1945, his comrades were weary, wounded, and worn, and they missed their families fiercely. One quiet Sunday evening, the chaplain gathered the troops in a makeshift chapel for a prayer meeting, and it was filled to overflowing. Solemn men praying solemn prayers, and there was one consistent theme expressed: that the war would end soon. "Please God, make this war come to an end."

Virgil tells me that it wasn't more than a day or two that the war did, in fact, come to an end. A siren sounded throughout the camp, and the announcement was made: "The campaign is finally over." And as you might expect, joyous celebration erupted among those weary troops. They screamed, they laughed, they wept, they hugged one another, and they partied well into the night. After supper that evening, Virg said that the chaplain invited all the troops back to the makeshift chapel, this time for a service of thanksgiving and praise to be held at 2100 hours. That is nine PM in military-speak. Perhaps the chaplain had a sneaking suspicion of what would occur, because at 9:15 PM, when only he and Private Johnson had gathered for prayer, the chaplain arose to read the Bible verses, this is what he read:

Now one of them, when he saw that he had been healed, turned back, glorifying God with a loud voice, and he fell on his face at the feet of Jesus, giving thanks to Him. And he was a Samaritan. Then Jesus answered and said, "Were there not ten cleansed ? But the nine – where are they? Was no one found who returned to give glory to God, except this foreigner ?"

I have heard it said that in foxholes there are no atheists. When the battle is raging, it seems like everyone calls upon God with urgent prayers. But when life returns to calm, the urgency is often forgotten, and people return to their self-centered ways.

In today's gospel lesson from Luke, Jesus has entered a conflicted zone. Both Jews and Samaritans occupied the border region between Samaria and Galilee, and you have heard before that Jews and Samaritans hated each other. We're not even sure why Jesus and his disciples are in this place, because Jesus was on his way to Jerusalem to die on the cross, and this region was a long way from Jerusalem.

When he entered a village, a gaggle of lepers approached him, crying out from a distance, "Jesus, master, have mercy on us!" There is a reason they called out to Jesus from a distance, because, as lepers, they were not allowed within the city walls, not allowed in the temple, and not even allowed to live in the homes of their families. "Unclean! Unclean!" They were required by Law to cry out "Unclean!" to give fair warning to any healthy persons that might be in the vicinity.

Leprosy was a dreadful disease. Patches of red rash began to appear, and then became oozing wounds. After awhile, fingers or toes would begin to decay and fall off from lack of circulation.

Worse than the disease, however, was the public shunning and humiliation they endured. Lepers were outcasts in the first order, and so they found each other and traveled in groups, if for no other reason than they needed each other for community. Well, there were ten of them, calling out to Jesus, that he might heal them. Interestingly, Jesus does not agree to heal them. Unlike the time he prepared mud and wiped it on the eyelids of the blind man, or licked his fingers and placed them in the ears and on the tongue of the deaf and dumb man, Jesus simply tells them to go and show themselves to the priests in the temple. And Luke tells us that, as they walked along, they began to notice that they were healed. No more blotchy skin. No more weeping sores. The ten became ecstatic. They screamed, they danced, and they hugged. And they ran to thank Jesus.

Well, not all of them. One of them. Only one turned back. The half-breed Samaritan went back to say thank you. Isn't it interesting that when they were lepers they needed each other? It didn't matter that they were of different ethnicity and different religions; no one else would have them, but at least they had each other. But now they didn't need their fellow lepers, so nine went north, and one went south. And the one who went south ran straight back to Jesus, singing and rejoicing and glorifying God all the way. And when he saw Jesus, he threw himself at the feet of the Lord and said thank you. Thank you. Thank you.

And Jesus then said, to no one in particular, "Hmmm. Didn't I heal ten lepers? Where are the other nine? The only one to say thanks was this foreigner?" And then he turned his eyes upon the man at his feet and he affirmed him. "Stand up and go home now, your faith has made you well." Jesus did not simply heal the man of his disease; he also reconciled the man to a healthy relationship with God and family. And all because the man said "thank you" to the one who made it possible.

Most Lutheran pastors offer three-point sermons, but I'm only giving two points today. You're welcome! The first point is this; we still live in a world where people are ostracized and shunned and then dismissed to the margins of life. It must somehow make us feel better about ourselves if we can point to someone else and think we are superior to him or her. It might be someone who is racially different than us, or who is economically poorer than us. We might think of ourselves as better than the one with less education, or the one who is smaller in stature, or the one who is less attractive and therefore, less valuable. James Dobson once said that in our American society, wealth is the gold coin of human worth, and beauty is the silver coin of human worth, and if you have either or both of those coins, you won't need anything else to be successful. Or maybe, because of our denomination, or because of our lifestyle, or because of our heritage, we conclude that God surely loves Swedish Lutherans more than he loves anyone else. And if you think that is true, then you will never understand how Jesus could love the Samaritan just as much as he loved the Jews. That Jesus would welcome the grateful Samaritan is proof that God doesn't measure people in the same way that we do. In fact, God doesn't measure people at all.

The second point of this two-point sermon on the ten lepers is the value Jesus places on gratitude. On that day in the border region of Samaria and Galilee, Jesus gave an enormous gift to ten men. He released them from their disease and therefore released them from the captivity of their shunning and their shame. What a gift! What a life-changing gift. He didn't instruct the lepers that, after they were certified as "cleansed" they should come back to say thank you. He didn't tell them that, for a gift so great as this, they should be grateful. Maybe he should have told them. The people of the world might need to be told to be grateful, but the people of God should not have to be told. For, of all people, we have received the most priceless gift that humankind has ever seen. Forgiveness for our sins? Reconciliation with God? Eternal life in the kingdom? Are you kidding me? Then we saunter through life as if we have earned it. As if we have deserved it.

So I'm wondering tonight, how long has it been since you have gotten down on your knees and thanked Jesus for dying on the cross for you? How recently have you seen a broken person and uttered the words "there, but for the grace of God, go I"? Somehow, we have misplaced the ability to express our thanks to God, except for one day a year, when we mostly thank him for turkey and football. For people that have been blessed, we surely ought to be more grateful to the source of our blessings. How could we do about doing that?

In the summer of 1982, former President Jimmy Carter was the keynote speaker at the National Lutheran Youth Assembly in Houston, Texas. Speaking before 35,000 young people, the President spoke about the blessing of growing up in a nation like ours, where freedom, and faith, and prosperity abound. But he closed his message with these words:

I know you are very young, but I want to leave you with these two questions: When was the last time you did an hour's worth of work for someone and didn't expect to be paid for it? And when was the last time you spent an hour on your knees, praying to the God who gave you everything you have, and everything you are?

Tonight, I would like to leave you with the same two questions. Have you served a neighbor in need lately, just because you can? And have you spent some time with Jesus, thanking him for every good gift in your life? Tonight, when you go to sleep, and tomorrow when you awaken, and wherever and with whomever you gather for a festive meal, may the first and last words out of your mouths be this: Thank you. Thank you. Thank you.

May it be so.

Amen.